*E*ASY TO MAKE

DOUGH CRAFTS

EASY TO MAKE

DOUGH CRAFTS

KRISTINA AGATE

BROCKHAMPTON PRESS
LONDON

First published in Great Britain in 1994
by Anaya Publishers Ltd, Strode House,
44-50 Osnaburgh Street, London NW1 3ND

This edition published 1995 by Brockhampton Press,
a member of Hodder Headline PLC Group
Reprinted 1996

Editor Helen Douglas Cooper
Design by Millions Design
Photographer Steve Tanner
Illustrations Pat Thorne

British Library Cataloguing in Publication Data
Agate, Kristina
Easy to Make Dough Crafts
I. Title
745.54

ISBN 1-86019-094-4

Typeset by Servis Filmsetting Ltd, Manchester, UK
Colour reproduction by Scantrans Pte Ltd, Singapore
Printed and bound in Hong Kong

CONTENTS

Introduction

In years gone by, modelling with salt dough was known as the poor man's craft, but now everyone enjoys it. The young and young-at-heart especially will find it fun.

The ancient Egyptians made dough figures to represent their gods and people in power. Bakers were seen as very important people in the community because bread was the population's main source of nourishment. There is a story that a young, forgetful baker once left a batch of dough lying in the midday sun. After several hours he discovered that his dough had become puffy. He was then curious to know what would happen if he was to bake it, and in doing so presented mankind with its first leavened loaf.

The beginning of intricate crafted bread dough began with the Spanish conquest in Equador and Bolivia. The Indians would craft their dough to imitate religious figures that had been introduced to them by the conquistadors.

To this day, the Spanish take sculpted bread to the graves of their ancestors and eat it in honour of the dead.

Many years later, the peasants made their own Christmas decorations out of dough. Unfortunately for them, the mice also enjoyed eating the decorations, so they added lots of salt to the dough to discourage them.

Today salt-dough models are given a coat of varnish to keep moisture out of the hardened dough and to give extra protection against hungry vermin.

Salt-dough making is a craft that anybody can experiment with. It is very frustrating when you have spent lots of money on an expensive new hobby, to find it all goes wrong. At least with salt-dough making you have not wasted a lot of money.

This book is filled with a variety of ways to use dough. It includes fun around the house where you can make door plates for children's rooms or a basket that you can fill with fruit or dried flowers. If you cannot afford to buy a beautiful Welsh dresser, why not make your own but in dough, not wood! There is a section on flower fun for those who enjoy the delicate touch, with instructions on making a wall garland. For those special dinner parties you can make candleholders, place cards and napkin rings to match.

There are salt-dough figures to suit all occasions, from Christmas to birthdays, and even ideas for that special gift for newly weds. For animal lovers there is a section on how to make Nellie the elephant, the three little pigs and a cuddly bear, and there are clowns and dolls to make for children.

Safety notes
Salt dough is made from organic ingredients, and is therefore safe to put in small mouths. As a mother of two small children, I can safely say that I have never seen a child put some in his or her mouth and enjoy it.

When young children are putting their models in the oven, it is essential that they are always guided by an adult. And always wear oven gloves when removing them from the oven or handling models that have just come out of the oven.

Use non-toxic paints for decorating the models, and wear protective clothing when varnishing them.

A lot of dogs enjoy baked salt dough as they make good chews, so keep them out of their reach, although no harm will come to them if they do have a chew.

Materials and techniques
The basic dough recipe is given in the Better Techniques section together with a list of the tools and equipment that are needed for all projects, plus general advice on handling the dough, baking it in the oven, and what to do if something goes wrong, such as the dough splitting or pieces dropping off. Advice is also given on painting and varnishing the models, and storing them safely.

Before making any of the models, read through the instructions carefully and make sure that you have all the materials and equipment you need close to hand.

All the projects in this book are fun to make. And the beauty is that often a slightly large nose or eyes set too close can be the making of a character. Nothing in this book has been measured to the exact millimetre. Dough is best modelled with the hands, unless you need to roll out a flat piece with a rolling-pin. It does not matter if your Easter rabbit collapses a little too far. It gives him his own happy, relaxed posture.

I experienced a very rewarding evening with a group of young girls, who showed me 20 different ways to make a teddy bear. Each bear was perfect, and every girl went home having enjoyed creating a masterpiece.

ONE

Fun Around the House

Door plates

These two door plates are made using plain and coloured dough. The bathroom plate should be hung on the outside of the door to protect it from moisture.

Materials
(For both plates)
4¾in (12cm) pastry cutter/compass and thick card
2lb (1kg) of plain dough (refer to Better Techniques)
Paints or food dyes: green, pink, pale blue, yellow, brown
5 small sandwich bags
Silver foil/non-stick baking paper
Garlic press
Toothpick
2 hooks

Preparation
1 If you do not have a pastry cutter, draw a 4¾in (12cm) circle on the card and cut out.

2 For the bathroom plate: Take ½lb (250g) of the dough, divide into 5 pieces, and knead a different colour into each (refer to Better Techniques). Place each in a plastic bag until required.

3 Trace off the flower and leaf shapes given here onto card and cut out.

Working the design
4 For each plate, roll out a handful of dough to ½in (1cm) thick and large enough to fill the circle. Transfer onto foil/baking paper and cut out two circles in the dough.

5 Prick all round the edge of the dough circles with a toothpick.

BEDROOM DOOR PLATE
6 Using ¼-palm of dough for each, make two oblongs 2in (5cm) long and place them in the middle of a dough circle.

7 The boy: For the head roll a ¼-finger of dough into a ball between your palms and position it above the right-hand body. Use a shaping tool to mark his pyjamas on the body piece.

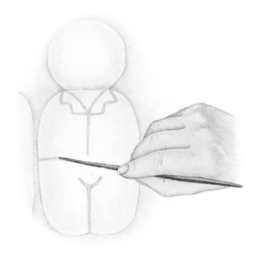

Mark the boy's pyjamas with a shaping tool

8 For his arm, roll a piece of dough into a sausage between your palms. Cut across one end on the diagonal and fix to the body. Roll very small balls for the buttons, nose and ear and fix in place. For the hair, push a piece of dough through a garlic press, and attach the strands starting at the side of his head and working up to the top.

Hanging door-plates
When hanging a door-plate, stick it to the door with double-sided tape. If the door slams, the tape will stop the model flying off and getting broken.

9 The teddy bear: Roll a ¼-finger of dough into a ball for the body. Use pieces half that size for the head, legs and arms. Roll tiny balls for the nose and ears. The bear's face is quite fiddly so make sure the dough is not too sticky.

10 Make the boy's feet from 2 bean-sized pieces of dough and press them up against the trouser bottoms.

11 The girl: For her nightie, roll out a piece of dough to ⅛in (5mm) thick and cut it out, checking that it is short enough to show her toes. Carefully lift the skirt into position and use the shaping tool to make creases for the waistband and pleats.

Cut out a piece of dough for the bath

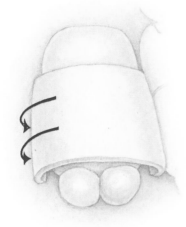

Cut out a piece of dough for the girl's skirt

Trace the flower and leaf on to card and cut out

12 Make the girl's head, arm, hair and feet in the same way as the boy's.

13 The rabbit: Follow the instructions for the teddy but give it long ears and a muzzle using two small balls of dough.

14 Make the eyes using a toothpick.

BATHROOM DOOR PLATE
15 Roll out a ¼-palm of dough to ⅛in (2.5mm) thick. Cut out the bath shape and position on a dough circle. Use a shaping tool to make the markings.

16 For the bears' heads roll a ¼-finger of dough into a ball between your palms for each, and position them above the bath. For their faces, shape a bean-sized piece of dough for each ear and press them into the head using a shaping tool. Use small fingertips of dough for the muzzles and pea-sized pieces for the noses. Make the eyes with a toothpick.

17 For the leaves and flowers, roll out the green dough thinly and place the leaf stencil on top. Cut round it with a sharp knife. Cut out the flowers in the same way from the pink and blue dough. Place the leaves down first. Press a blunt pencil into the middle of the flowers and position them on top of the leaves. Add a tiny ball of dough in the centre of each.

18 For the bubbles, roll pea-sized pieces of dough into balls, and place them around the bears and bath.

19 Bake in the oven for at least 6 hours or until rock hard, adding the hook after 1 hour (refer to Better Techniques).

Finishing
20 When cold, paint the plates, paint in the features on the faces, and varnish them.

Welsh dresser

The Welsh dresser looks especially nice hanging on the kitchen wall. You can paint the jars and pots to match those in your own kitchen.

Materials

2lb (1kg) of plain dough – chapatti flour
can be used for a grainier effect (refer
to Better Techniques)
Stiff card
Silver foil/non-stick baking paper
16 cloves
Hook

Preparation

1 Trace the plate and heart shapes given
here on to card and cut out.

Trace the plate and heart shapes on to card and
cut out

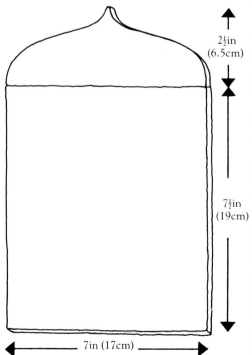

2½in (6.5cm)

7½in (19cm)

7in (17cm)

Cut out the main shape for the dresser

Working the design

2 Roll out all the dough into a long
oblong approximately 7 × 11in
(17 × 28cm) and ½in (1cm) thick. Transfer
on to silver foil/baking paper. Using a
kitchen knife, cut out the dresser shape
following the dimensions given.

3 Roll out a handful of dough to 2 × 5½in
(5 × 14cm) and ½in (1cm) thick and place
it along the bottom to make the
cupboards. Using a shaping tool, mark
the grooves and around the heart stencil.

4 For the side panels, cut out 2 pieces of
dough 1 × 7½in (1.5 × 19cm) and ½in (1cm)
thick, and place these down either side.

5 For the shelves, cut out a piece of
dough 1 × 5½in (2 × 14cm) and ½in (1cm)
thick. Cut it in half lengthways to give 2
pieces ½in (1cm) wide and position them.

6 Groove the top part of the dresser
using the shaping tool, and cut out the
heart shape using the stencil. Use 12 of
the cloves to decorate the top edge.

7 To make the plates, use a palm of
dough rolled out to about ¼in (5mm)
thick. Cut them out using the plate
stencil and use the smaller circle to mark
the centre of the plates.

8 Make the pots by rolling out pieces of
dough into various shapes and sizes.

9 Make the fruit bowl from a 2¼in (6cm)-
thick sausage and press it down into the
cupboard. Form the apples, pears and
plums by rolling small pieces of dough
between your palm and forefinger and
place them in the bowl. Press a clove into
each apple and pear for the stalks.

10 Bake in the oven for 12 hours or until
rock hard, fixing the hook in place after 2
hours (refer to Better Techniques).

Finishing

11 When cold, paint the items on the
shelves, and varnish the whole dresser.

Teddy bear family

This colourful family of bears hangs on the wall, and the figures can be altered to suit any family of your choice. They are painted after baking.

Materials

Stiff card

2lb (1kg) of plain dough made with chapatti flour (refer to Better Techniques)

3in (8cm) pastry cutter

Silver foil/non-stick baking paper

Flower press or felt-tip pen lid (refer to Better Techniques)

Hook

Preparation

1 Trace the flower stencil given here on to card and cut out.

Working the design

2 For the bodies of the large bears take 2 large handfuls of dough and knead them into round balls. Then roll them out into fat oblongs. Place them side by side, pressing them together gently.

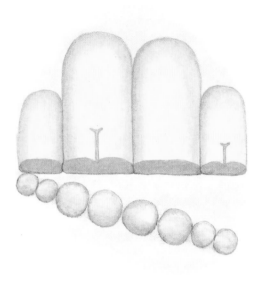

Cut across the bottom of the 4 body pieces and attach a pair of feet to each body.

3 For the small bears, take 2 ½-palms of dough and repeat step 2. Position them on either side of the large bears, making sure the four pieces line up along the bottom. The four body pieces should stick together to form one piece.

4 Using a kitchen knife, cut off ¾in (1.5cm) across the bottom.

5 Mark the dough with a crafting knife for the father's and boy's legs.

6 For the large bears' heads, roll a ½-palm of dough into a ball between your palms for each. Place them in position and press gently against the tops of the heads to attach them to the bodies. Shape a bean-sized piece of dough for each ear and press them into the heads using the shaping tool. Use a small fingertip of dough for each muzzle and pea-sized pieces for the noses. Make the eyes with a toothpick.

7 To make the ribbing on the father's jumper, roll out a long sausage and flatten it using the palm of your hand. Cut a ½in (1cm) wide strip long enough to

go across his stomach, and another for his neck. Use the shaping tool to press into the dough to make ribbing.

8 For the large bears' arms, roll a ½-palm of dough into a sausage, and cut in half on the diagonal. Attach the cut ends on either side of the figures.

9 Roll 2 small pieces of dough between your palms for the small bears' heads. Press into the elbow area on each side of the large bears with your thumb and position the small bears' heads there. Press the heads down to fix them to the bodies. Make their faces as for the large bears.

10 Make the small bears' arms using a ¼-palm of dough rolled into a sausage 2¼in (6cm) long. Cut it in half on the diagonal and place the cut ends against the sides of the small bears.

11 To make the hat, roll out a piece of dough to ½in (1cm) thick. Cut out a circle with the pastry cutter. From this cut a

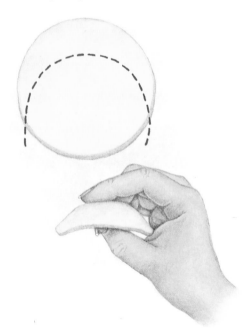

Cut out a piece of dough for the hat brim

half-moon shape with a small knife for the brim, and position it across the front of the head. For the crown of the hat, take an oblong of dough and press it up in the middle with your thumbs. Place it behind the brim. Using the stencil, cut out the flower from a piece of dough rolled out to ¼in (5mm) thick. Position them and place a tiny ball of dough in the centre of each.

12 To make the bow, roll out the dough on a floured surface to ¼in (5mm) thick. Cut a strip ½in (1cm) wide and 1½in (4cm) long, and then cut to shape. Push into the dough with the shaping tool to form the knot, and mark little creases on either side of it. Cut 2 thin strips of dough for the ribbons and position them under the bow.

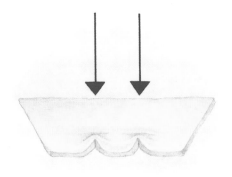

Cut out a piece of dough for the bow

13 Make the linked arms with a ½-palm of dough. Roll it into a sausage 2¾in (7cm) long, and cut through it diagonally 2in (5cm) from one end. Lay the longer piece across the father bear's chest, then lay the shorter one over it.

14 For the feet, roll small balls of dough and gently press them up against the bodies.

Trace the flower on to card and cut out

15 To make the flowers on the dresses cut out small discs of dough, fix them in place, and then press into each with a flower press or an interesting felt-tip pen top.

16 Bake in the oven for 15 hours or until rock hard.

Finishing
17 When cold, paint the bears' clothes and features, and varnish the whole family.

Painting details
For faces, paint a thin dark line over each eye for the eyebrow, and two thick, looped lines under the nose for the mouth.

Clothes look much more interesting if they are painted with some sort of pattern, rather than being just plain colours. Vary the colours and patterns for each figure, using spots, stripes, check patterns and flowers. You can base the clothes on the favourite things worn by your family or friends.

Door for keys

This door is designed to hold your keys. It hangs on the wall by your front door, and you can hang up your keys on the gold-coloured hooks when you arrive home.

Materials
1½lb (750g) of plain dough (refer to Better Techniques)
Silver foil/non-stick baking paper
Tool for making roof pattern
3 gold hooks
Hook

Working the design
1 Roll out 1½ handfuls of dough to ½in (1cm) thick and large enough to cut out a rectangle 4¾ × 5in (12 × 13cm). Transfer to silver foil/baking paper and cut out the rectangle. Mark a line along the top and down the sides ¾in (1.5cm) in from the edges with a shaping tool.

2 Roll out a handful of dough to ¼in (5mm) thick and cut out a rectangle 3½ × 2in (9 × 5cm). Position this on the door ¾in (1.5cm) from the top. Use a shaping tool to frame the sides of the rectangle. Fix a ball of dough on to the door for the door knob.

3 Roll out a handful of dough to ½in (1cm) thick and cut out a triangle. The base should be slightly wider than the door. Place it above the door and mark the wooden panel effect on it with a shaping tool.

4 Make the triangular frame at the top by rolling out 2 narrow strips of dough 3½in (9cm) long. Place on the triangle, and cut the ends so that they fit together at the top. Press a shaping tool or patterned tool into the strips to create a decorative effect.

5 Roll out a piece of dough for the base of the door ½in (1cm) thick, 6½in (16cm) long and 2in (5cm) deep. Position it across the bottom of the door and cut it to fit the door frame. Push the 3 hooks into the base of the door.

6 Bake for 10 hours or until rock hard, adding the hook at the back after 2 hours (refer to Better Techniques). It is very important that it is allowed to cool down slowly.

Finishing
7 When cold, decorate the door and varnish it.

> **Avoiding the damp**
> Don't put a doughcraft model anywhere damp such as against a damp wall or in a porch, because the moisture will get into it and it will go soft.

Fit the angled ends of the dough together to form the top of the triangular frame

Mermaid

This bathroom door plate is full of detail. The mermaid, fish, plants, shells and starfish are easy to make and all fit nicely onto a rolled-out piece of dough.

Materials
Stiff card
2lb (1kg) of plain dough (refer to Better Techniques)
Silver foil/non-stick baking paper
Garlic press
Hook

Preparation
1 Trace the seaweed, shell and starfish stencils on to card and cut out.

Working the design
2 Take 1lb (500g) of the dough and knead it to get rid of any air bubbles. Roll out an oblong approximately $8\frac{3}{4} \times 7$in (22 × 18cm) and $\frac{1}{2}$in (1cm) thick.

Transfer it on to silver foil/baking paper. Cut off the corners to create an oval, and smooth the edges with a wet finger.

3 To make the mermaid's body, take a handful of dough and roll it into a sausage. The top half should be $1\frac{1}{2}$in (4cm) thick, the tail end approximately $\frac{3}{4}$in (1.5cm). Curl the body around and position it on the dough plate.

4 For the head, roll a $\frac{1}{2}$-palm of dough into a ball and fix it above the body.

5 Make the arms from a $\frac{1}{2}$-palm of dough. Roll it into a sausage, and cut in half on the plate against the body piece,

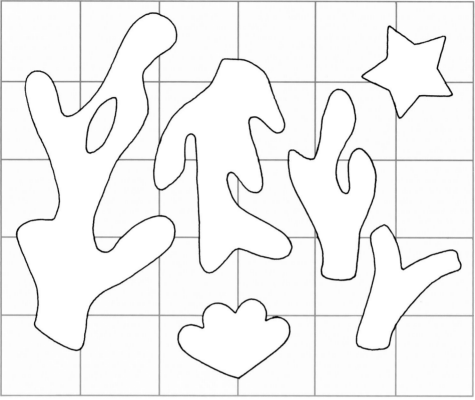

Trace the seaweed, shell and starfish shapes on to card and cut out

and place the right arm across the mermaid's chest.

6 Roll out a palm of dough to ½in (1cm) thick and cut out two tail shapes. Make fin markings with a shaping tool. Fix the tail pieces on either side of the end of the body, overlapping the side of the plate. Use the shaping tool to mark where the tail begins.

7 Roll out a piece of dough to ¼in (5mm) thick. Place the seaweed stencil on top of the dough and cut around it. Fix it in position. Do the same for the shells and starfish.

8 Form the blue-and-yellow fish from a ¼-palm of dough. Roll it into a ball, and then press into it using your finger and thumb to create its head. Position the fins and tail using the shaping tool. Cut the red-and-white fish from a ½in (1cm)

thick piece of dough and use a shaping tool to attach its fins.

9 Make the hair by pressing pieces of dough through the garlic press. Several layers will be needed to form the long, flowing effect. Build up the layers from the bottom, adding those around her face last. Use a tiny ball of dough for the nose.

10 Make the pearl and bubbles from small balls of dough rolled between a finger and the palm of your hand.

11 Bake for 10 hours or until rock hard, adding the hook after 2 hours (refer to Better Techniques). Cool down very slowly.

Finishing
12 When cold, paint the plate and varnish it.
NB Don't hang it on walls that are damp.

21

TWO

Flower Fun

Garland of flowers

The dough is gathered and folded to make layers of grace and charm. The garland is made from both plain and coloured dough and hangs on the wall.

Materials
2lb (1kg) of plain dough (refer to Better Techniques)
Paints or food dyes: green, red, pink, peach, white, yellow
6 small sandwich bags
Stiff card
Compass
Silver foil/non-stick baking paper
Toothpick
Hook

Preparation
1 Take ½lb (250g) of the dough and divide into 6 pieces. Knead a colour into each piece and store in the sandwich bags until you need them (refer to Better Techniques).

2 Trace the flower and leaf stencils given here on to card and cut out. Using the compass, draw a 6½in (16cm) diameter circle on the card and cut out.

Working the design

3 Take 1½ handfuls of plain dough and roll out on a lightly floured surface to ½in (1cm) thick. Transfer on to silver foil/baking paper and cut out a piece 8¾ × 7½in (22 × 19cm).

4 Scrunch the dough together at each end to form the folds of the garland. Use a crafting knife to add a few extra folds.

5 Take 1 handful of plain dough and roll out to ½in (1cm) thick. Place the card circle on top of the dough and cut it out. Cut the circle in half and gather up each straight edge. Place the pieces on either side of the main garland. Use a pattern tool to decorate the edges.

6 Make two strips of dough 3 × 1in (8 × 2cm) and wrap one over each join between the central and side pieces to seal them together.

7 Leaves and flowers: Attach the leaves first, and then the flowers. Make the leaves from the green dough and flowers from the other colours using the stencils. Roll out the dough to ¼in (5mm) thick. Place the stencil on top and cut round with a small knife. To position a flower, place it on your finger and press into the middle with a blunt pencil, then place it where you want it. Roll a tiny ball of dough and place it in the centre of the flower.

Trace the flower and leaf shapes on to card and cut out

8 The large primrose-shaped flowers and the roses are modelled. For the primrose shape, flatten 5 pea-size pieces of dough between your fingers. Place them around the flower centre, which is a small, thin sausage of dough. Fold the petals around the thin sausage. For the rose shape, roll out a piece of dough to $\frac{1}{16}$in (1mm) thick and cut a strip ½in (1cm) wide and 1½in (4cm) long. Using your finger, gently roll up the strip of dough. With your fingertips, carefully separate the layers of petals. Place the end of a toothpick into the centre of the flower and press the flower into position on the figure. Make a small hole so that the rose sits nicely.

9 Bake for 10 hours or until rock hard, adding the hook after 2 hours (refer to Better Techniques).

Finishing
When cold, varnish the garland.

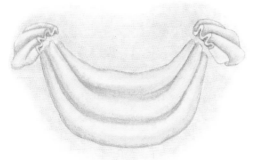

Scrunch up the ends of the dough to form folds

Candleholder

This easy to make candleholder complements any dinner party table. Choose the colours to match your tableware. It is made from plain and coloured dough.

Materials
(For two candleholders)
1lb (500g) of plain dough (refer to Better Techniques)
Paints or food dyes: red, pink, green, yellow
4 small sandwich bags
Stiff card
Silver foil/non-stick baking paper
2 candles

Preparation
1 Take 4¼lb (125g) of the dough and divide into 4 pieces. Knead a colour into each and store in the plastic bags (refer to Better Techniques).

2 Trace the flower and leaf stencils given here on to card and cut out.

Working the design
3 Take a handful of plain dough and roll it into a ball. Transfer it on to silver foil/baking paper and press down on it gently with the palm of your hand.

4 Take the candle and press it down ¾in (2cm) into the top of the dough. Wiggle the candle about so that the hole is a little larger than the candle (the dough will shrink when baked).

5 Leaves and flowers: Attach the leaves and then the flowers to the candleholder starting at the base. Make the leaves from the green dough and the flowers from the pink and red dough using the stencils. Roll out the dough to ¼in (5mm) thick. Place the stencil on top and cut round with a small knife. To position a flower, place it on your fingers and press into the middle with a blunt pencil, then place it

where you want it. Roll a tiny ball of dough and place it in the centre of the flower. For the rose shape, roll out a piece of dough to $\frac{1}{16}$in (1mm) thick and cut a strip ½in (1cm) wide and 1½in (4cm) long. Using your finger, gently roll up the strip of dough. With your fingertips, carefully separate the layers of petals. Place the end of a toothpick into the centre of the flower and press the flower into position on the figure. Make a small hole so that the rose sits nicely.

6 Bake for at least 8 hours or until rock hard.

Finishing
7 Varnish when cold. To fix the candle into the holder, light the candle first and let the wax drip into the hole. While the wax is still hot, place the candle into the hole and hold it there until the wax has set, to keep it upright.

Trace the leaf and flower shapes on to card and cut out

26

Napkin ring and place card

Napkin rings and place cards brighten any table setting. Use napkins in a matching colour. You can use sticky labels on the place cards and renew them on each occasion.

Materials
1lb (500g) of plain dough (refer to Better Techniques)
Paints or food dyes: red, green
2 small sandwich bags
Stiff card
Empty toilet roll
Straw
Silver foil/non-stick baking paper
Toothpick

Preparation
1 Take ¼lb (125g) of the dough and divide in half. Knead red into 1 piece and green into the other, and store in the plastic bags (refer to Better Techniques).

2 Trace the leaf stencil given here on to card and cut out.

3 Cut out a piece of card 4¼ × 5½in (11 × 14cm) and fold in half.

Working the design

NAPKIN RING
1 Take a handful of plain dough and roll it out to ½in (1cm) thick and 7¾in (20cm) long. Cut out a strip 2 × 6¾in (5 × 17cm). Cut off the corners at one end to round it off. Place on silver foil/baking paper.

2 Carefully roll the dough over the toilet roll, leaving the rounded end free. Make sure it is secure at the join.

3 Decorate along both side edges of the napkin ring and round the end with the end of the straw.

4 The leaves: Make 5 leaves from the green dough. Roll out the dough to ¼in

Wrap the dough around a loo roll

Trace the leaf on to card and cut out

(5mm) thick. Place the stencil on top and cut round with a small knife. Place 3 leaves on top of the napkin ring and two on the free end.

5 The strawberries: Roll 3 bean-sized pieces of dough into balls and place on top of the leaves. Gently press into them with the toothpick to make the strawberry markings.

6 Take 2 very small slithers of green dough and roll them out thinly, making sure the ends are pointed. Cross them over the top of each strawberry and press into the middle with a toothpick.

PLACE CARD

7 Roll out a handful of plain dough and cut out an oblong 4 × 5in (10 × 13cm). Place it over the folded piece of card and stand on silver foil.

8 Make the leaves and strawberries following the instructions above. Place the leaves in position first, and the strawberries on top, on one top corner of the place card.

9 Bake for 6 hours or until rock hard, removing the toilet roll and piece of card after 2 hours.

Finishing
10 Varnish when cold.

Basket of flowers

This pretty basket of flowers hangs on the wall. It is made from plain and coloured dough, and is decorated with several different kinds of flowers.

Materials
2lb (1kg) of plain dough (refer to Better Techniques)
Paints or food dyes: red, pink, green, light blue, dark blue, yellow
6 small sandwich bags
Stiff card
Silver foil/non-stick greaseproof paper
Hook

Preparation
1 Take ½lb (250g) of the dough and divide into 6 pieces. Knead a colour into each and store in the plastic bags until you are ready to use them (refer to Better Techniques).

2 Trace the flowers and leaf stencils given here on to card and cut out.

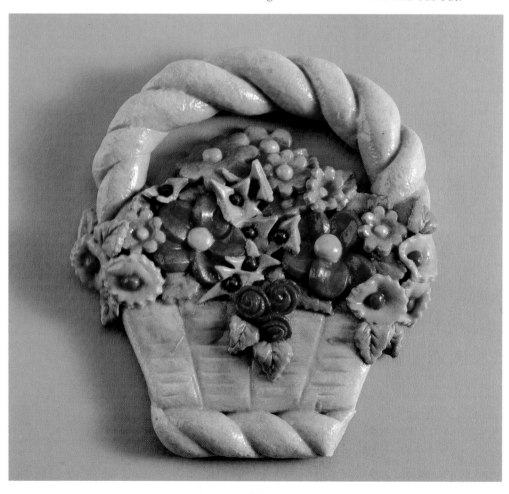

Twist the 2 lengths of dough for the handle

$\frac{1}{4}$in (5mm) thick. Place the stencils on top and cut round with a small knife. For each rose, cut a strip of red dough $\frac{1}{2}$in (1cm) wide and 1$\frac{1}{2}$in (4cm) long. Roll it up and gently separate the layers.

9 To decorate the basket, first place the leaves around the outer edge. Then attach the red flowers, next add the blue, then the pink, and finally the yellow (refer to Better Techniques). Add a tiny ball of dough in the centre of each flower, with a few extra leaves around the bottom flowers.

10 Bake for 10 hours or until rock hard, adding the hook after 2 hours (refer to Better Techniques).

Finishing
11 When cold, varnish.

Trace the leaf and flower shapes on to card and cut out

Working the design
3 Roll out a large handful of plain dough to $\frac{1}{2}$in (1cm) thick and transfer on to silver foil/baking paper.

4 Using a small kitchen knife, cut out the basket shape.

5 Take another handful of plain dough and divide into 2. Roll each one between your palms to make two sausages approximately 13$\frac{1}{4}$in (35cm) long. Starting at one end, twist them together.

6 Cut a strip of the twisted dough long enough to go round the bottom of the basket. Curve the remaining twist above the basket and attach at each side.

7 Take a palm of dough and press it into the top of the basket.

8 Make the leaves from the green dough and the flowers apart from the roses using the stencils. Roll out the dough to

Attach a piece of dough to the top of the basket

31

Basket of Fruit

The wealth of shapes and colours to be found at a fruit counter provided the inspiration for this rich fruit basket, the perfect decoration for a kitchen wall.

Materials
Stiff card
1½lb (750g) of plain dough (refer to Better Techniques)
Silver foil/non-stick baking paper
7 cloves

Preparation
1 Trace the leaf stencil given here on to card and cut out.

Method
2 Take a handful of dough and roll out to a thickness of ½in (1cm) on a lightly floured table. Transfer onto silver foil/baking paper.

3 Using a small kitchen knife, cut out the basket shape. This is 6in (15cm) long at the top with 3½in (9cm) sides, sloping to a base 2in (5cm). With the shaping tool, mark the basket's weave lines.

4 Make 2 pears by rolling ½-finger of dough into a ball. Using your finger, gently roll one end of the ball slightly flatter. Place onto the basket as shown in the picture.

5 Make 2 apples and 2 oranges using ½-finger of dough rolled into balls. Make a smaller ball of dough for the 3rd orange. Arrange on the basket as in the picture.

6 For the plums, take ¼-fingers of dough and roll into small oval shapes. With the shaping tool, make a line down the middle of each. Place on the basket as shown in the picture.

7 For the grapes, roll about 35 small pellets of dough into slightly oblong balls. Place on either side of the basket to form bunches.

8 Push a clove into each pear and apple, head end first. Put cloves into the oranges stalk end first, pushing the cloves into the dough up to the head.

9 To make the handle, take a handful of dough and divide into 2. Roll each piece between your palms to make 2 sausages approximately 12in (30cm) long. Starting at one end, twist them together.

10 Trim both ends of the twisted length. Place one end on the top right hand edge of the basket behind the fruit. Curve the length into a handle and position the other end 2½in (6cm) in from the top left-hand edge of the basket, over the fruit.

11 To make the leaves, roll out the remaining dough to ¼in (5mm) thick. Place the stencil on top and cut around using a small kitchen knife. Mark leaf veins on the cut-out shapes using the shaping tool. Position the leaves around the fruit and over the base of the handle to hide the join.

Leaf stencil

Finishing

12 Bake in the oven for 8 hours or until rock hard. When cold, paint the fruit and leaves as shown. Once the paint has dried, varnish.

Variations

You can alter the types of fruit you use to decorate the basket. Cherries and strawberries, for example, provide colourful alternatives. Make cherries by rolling small balls of dough and then group them together on the basket. Strawberries are made by rolling bean-sized pieces of dough into a strawberry shape. Then mark them with a toothpick. You could also vary the shape of the leaves, making some longer and thinner.

THREE

Festive Fun

Father Christmas

Here is Father Christmas with his sack of toys. He hangs on the wall at Christmas. For the rest of the year he should be wrapped and stored in a damp-free place.

Materials
2lb (1kg) of plain dough (refer to Better
   Techniques)
Silver foil/non-stick baking paper
Garlic press
Toothpick
Hook

Working the design
1 Take 1 large handful of dough and mould into a 4in (10cm) oblong. Transfer on to silver foil/baking paper.

2 Using a shaping tool, mark the position of the legs. Then cut ½in (1cm) off the bottom.

3 For the head, take a palm of dough and roll it into a ball between your palms. Place it above the body and press gently to fix them together.

4 You need only make the coat from the belt down. Take a palm of dough and make a sausage about 2¾in (7cm) long. Roll it out to ¼in (5mm) thick. Cut out a strip 1in (2cm) deep and 4¾in (12cm) wide. Lay it across his stomach. Using the shaping tool, press gently round the top ½in (1cm) to make the belt. Make the fur trimming in the same way from a strip of dough ½in (1cm) deep. Use the shaping tool to create the fur effect.

5 For the arms, roll a sausage of dough and cut it in half on the diagonal. Fix the angled ends to the sides of the body and cut off the arms at the wrists to make sleeves. Press into the arms with the shaping tool ½in (1cm) above the wrists to make cuffs. Press into the cuffs to create a fur effect. Add balls of dough for hands.

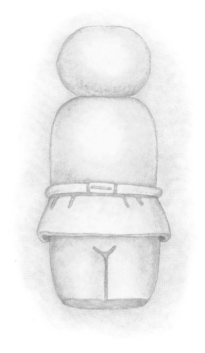

Mark the legs with a shaping tool

6 To make the beard and hair, press pieces of dough through the garlic press. Start building up the beard in the middle and work up round the face. Add a tiny ball of dough for the nose, and position the moustache last. Make the eyes with the toothpick.

7 Make the hat from a palm of dough rolled out to ¼in (5mm) thick. Cut out a triangle and fold it over his head, holding on to the tip, and then fold the tip over to one side. Place a ½-finger of dough rolled into a ball at the tip and create a fur effect on it.

8 The boots are made from 2 ½-palms of dough rolled into balls. Using your thumb, press them against the legs to flatten them slightly. The feet are made with a ¼-palm of dough and attached in the same way. Make more fur trimming and lay it across the top of the boots. Press it in the middle to separate them.

9 For the sack, roll out a rough circle using a palm of dough. Fold in the edges and squash them together at one end. Place that end by his hand. Then roll a ¼-finger of dough into a ball and squeeze at one edge. Mark creases on it on the opposite side and place it on top of his hand.

10 Bake for 12 hours or until rock hard, adding the hook after 2 hours (refer to Better Techniques).

Finishing
11 When cold, paint the clothes and hair, paint on the features, and varnish the whole hanging.

Angel with cloud

The happy angel leaning on a white fluffy cloud decorated with stars watches over the children as they sleep, the day before Father Christmas arrives. She hangs on the wall.

Materials
1½lb (750g) of plain dough (refer to Better
  Techniques)
Stiff card
Silver foil/non-stick baking paper
Garlic press
Picture wire
Toothpick

Preparation
1 Trace the star and wing stencils given
here on to card and cut out.

Working the design
2 Take a large handful of dough and
mould into a flat oblong 5in (13cm) wide
for the cloud, and transfer on to silver
foil/baking paper. Use your fingers and
thumb to make the cloud texture.

3 For the head, roll a palm of dough into
a ball between your palms and place on
top of the cloud. Add a tiny blob of
dough for the nose.

4 The wings are made by rolling out a
palm of dough to ¼in (5mm) thick. Lay
the wing shape stencil on top and cut
round with a small knife. Reverse stencil
and repeat. Use a shaping tool to make
the wing veins, and place on either side
of the head.

5 For the arms, make 2 2in (5cm) long
sausages and place them on either side of
her face. Use the shaping tool to mark

her thumbs. Don't neaten the joins as her
hair will cover them. Use the shaping
tool to mark where her sleeves end.

6 To make the hair, push pieces of
dough through the garlic press. Attach
the longest strands first, and build up the
hair working up around her face.

7 A small sausage 1½in (4cm) long and ⅛in
(2.5cm) thick makes her halo. Join the
two ends together and place on top of
her hair.

8 Cut 4 pieces of picture wire: 2¾in
(7cm), 2¼in (6cm), 2in (5cm) and 1½in
(4cm). Push the 2¼in (6cm) piece into the
left-hand end of the cloud, then the 2¾in
(7cm) piece, then the 1½in (4cm) piece,
and finally the 2in (5cm) piece all
approximately 1in (2cm) apart.

9 Roll out the dough to 5mm (¼in) thick.
Cut out 4 stars using the stencil.

10 Bake, including the stars, for 1 hour.
Carefully push the ends of the wires into
the stars (if you try to insert the wire
while the stars are soft, they may lose
their shape). Bake for a further 10 hours,
or until rock hard, adding the hook after
a further hour (refer to Better
Techniques).

Finishing
11 When cold, paint, put in the features
and varnish.

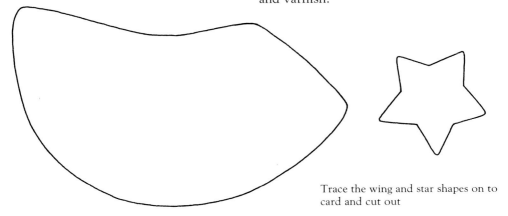

Trace the wing and star shapes on to
card and cut out

Christmas decorations

Give your house a more original look at Christmas time by making your own decorations. These can hang on the Christmas tree or on the wall.

SNOWMEN
Materials
1 palm of plain dough (refer to Better Techniques)
Silver foil/non-stick baking paper
Toothpick
1½in (4cm) of thin decorative string

Working the design
1 Roll 2 ¾-fingers of dough and place together for the bodies. Transfer on to silver foil/baking paper.

2 Roll 2 ¼-fingers of dough into balls between your palms for the heads and place on top of the bodies.

3 For the hats, shape 2 ¼-fingers of dough into triangles and place above the heads. Add 2 pea-sized pieces of dough for the bobbles.

4 Roll out a finger of dough and cut out two strips ½in (1cm) wide. Wrap these round the necks and trim. Use the leftover pieces to form the scarf ends and mould the tassels with a shaping tool or toothpick.

5 Add tiny balls of dough for the noses and use the toothpick to make the eyes.

HOLLY TREE
Materials
1 palm of plain dough
Stiff card
Silver foil/non-stick baking paper
1½in (4cm) of thin decorative string

Preparation
1 Trace the holly stencil given here on to stiff card and cut out.

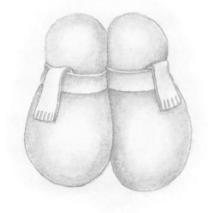

Use a shaping tool to make the scarves

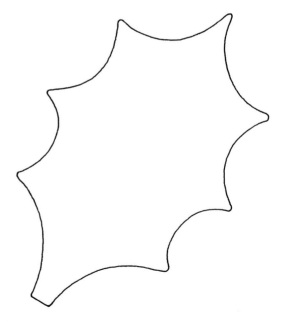

Trace the holly shape on to card and cut out

40

2 Roll pieces of silver foil into 4 loose balls about 1cm (½in) in diameter.

Working the design
3 Roll out the green dough on a lightly floured surface to 1cm (½in) thick. Lay the holly stencil on top and with a sharp knife cut out 4 leaves. Mark a central vein on each leaf using the shaping tool.

4 Arrange the leaves on a sheet of silver foil/baking paper and join them in the middle. Place a ball of silver foil under each leaf to make it curl.

5 Roll pea-sized pieces of dough into balls and place on top of the holly leaves.

6 Bake the decorations for 4 hours or until rock hard.

Finishing
7 When cold paint and varnish the decorations. Tie loops of decorative string and fix to the backs of the decorations with strong glue, first checking that the decoration will hang straight.

Note: Do not make Christmas tree decorations too heavy or large, or they will fall off.

41

Snowman

This jolly snowman surrounded by snowballs sits on the table, and is decorated on all sides. It is made in two stages and is painted after baking.

Materials

1½lb (750g) of plain dough (refer to Better
   Techniques)
Silver foil/non-stick baking paper
Pastry cutter
Toothpick

Working the design

1 For the body, take a large handful of
dough and roll it into a ball. Place it on
silver foil/baking paper.

2 Take a palm of dough and roll it into a
ball. Make sure the dough is not too wet
or it will slide off the top. If necessary,
add more flour to the dough mixture.
Place the small ball on top of the large
ball to form the head.

3 Bake in the oven for 2 hours, until the
dough has crusted, to give yourself a firm
base to work on. Don't let the snowman
get cold while you're working on it.

4 For the hat, roll out a ½-palm of dough
to ⅛in (2.5mm) thick, and cut out a circle
with the pastry cutter (use it upside down
if it has a pinking edge). Decorate round
the edge of the circle with a shaping tool.

Cut out a piece of dough for the rim of the hat

5 Mould a round ball of dough with
your fingers and place it on top of the
snowman's head. Then place the hat over
the ball of dough and secure it to the
head using the shaping tool.

6 For the scarf, roll a palm of dough into
a 3½in (9cm) sausage and roll it out to
make a long, flat sausage about ⅛in
(2.5mm) thick and 12in (30cm) long.
Wrap it around the neck. Add a 1in
(2cm) strip to the side of the head, so that
it looks as if the scarf has been folded
over.

Cross over the ends of the strip of dough for the
scarf

7 The bobble, nose and snowballs are
made from pea-sized pieces of dough.
Use plenty of water to fix the snowballs
in place to make sure that they stick
together. The eyes are made with the
toothpick.

8 Bake for at least 8 hours, or until rock
hard.

Finishing

9 Paint once the snowman has cooled,
and varnish it.

Birthday number

Happy Birthday 5-year-old! You are only five once so celebrate and remember your day with an easy-to-make number. The design can be adapted to suit any anniversary.

Materials
1½lb (750g) of plain dough (refer to Better Techniques)
Stiff card
Silver foil/non-stick baking paper
Toothpick
Hook

Preparation
1 Trace the 5 (or the appropriate number) given here on to thick card and cut out.

Working the design
2 Roll out a handful of dough to ¾in (2cm) thick. Transfer on to silver foil/baking paper. Place the 5 stencil on top of the dough and cut out using a small knife.

3 For the candles (optional), roll out a palm of dough to ¾in (1.5cm) thick and 2in (5cm) long. Cut 5 strips for the candles ½in (1cm) wide, and place along the top edge ¼in (5mm) apart. The flames are pea-sized pieces of dough pinched between the fingers while being put in place.

4 The birthday presents are ¾in (1.5cm) square pieces of dough. Make the

ribbons by pressing into the dough with a shaping tool.

5 To make each bear, roll a ¼-finger of dough into a ball for the body. Use pieces half that size for the head, legs and arms. Roll small balls for the nose and ears. The bear's face is quite fiddly so make sure the dough is not too sticky. To make the bow ties, roll out the dough to ¼in (5mm) thick. Cut a small strip and then cut it to shape. Push into the dough with the shaping tool to form the knot, and mark creases on either side of it.

6 The balloons are ¾in (1.5cm) long. For each, roll a ball of dough, place it on the 5, and mould it into shape with your fingers. Use the shaping tool to mark the knots. The strings are made from pea-sized pieces of dough rolled between the fingertips.

7 Bake for 10 hours or until rock hard, adding the hook after 2 hours (refer to Better Techniques).

Finishing
8 Paint and varnish when cold.

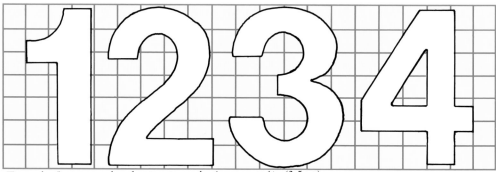

Trace the 5 on to card and cut out – scale: 1 square = 1in (2.5cm)

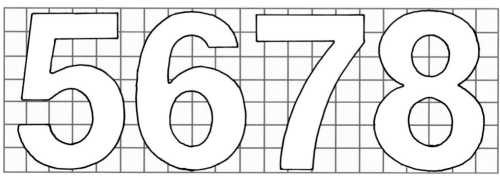

Easter bunnies

These two Easter bunnies sit on a table. They are supported by a straight glass while being modelled, and are made from plain and coloured dough.

Materials
2lb (1kg) of plain dough (refer to Better
  Techniques)
Paints or food dyes: pink, pale blue,
  yellow, red, green, peach
6 small plastic sandwich bags
Silver foil/non-stick baking paper
1 tall, straight glass, oiled
Toothpick

Preparation
1 Take ½lb (250g) of the dough and divide
into 6 pieces. Knead a colour into each
and store in plastic bags (refer to Better
Techniques).

Working the design
2 Place the glass on the silver foil/baking
paper.

3 For the bodies, take 2 palm-sized
pieces of dough and shape them into fat
oblongs. Using your thumbs, press into
the middle of each to bend them. Place
them on the silver foil/baking paper and
prop them against the glass.

Press into the body pieces with your thumbs to
make them sit

4 For the heads, roll 2 ½-palms of dough
into balls between the palms of your
hands. Place them on the bodies and rest
them against each other to give support.

5 Make the 2 outside arms by rolling a
sausage of dough, and cutting it in half
on the diagonal. Fix the angled ends to
the bodies. Make the 2 pairs of legs in
the same way from 2 fatter sausages.

6 For the linked arms, make 1 arm as
before and cut in 2 on the diagonal ¾ of
the way along it. Attach the longer arm
across one body and the smaller arm over
it.

7 Make the ears from 4 sausages, 1½in
(4cm) long and ¾in (1.5cm) wide. Cut off
¼in (5mm) from the base of each, and
pinch the tops between your fingertips.
Position them on top of the heads and
use a shaping tool to make the lobes.

8 Make the muzzles from pea-sized
pieces of dough, and press them together
when you position them. Make the noses
from tiny pieces of red dough rolled into
a ball and position them above the
muzzles.

9 Use the toothpick to make the eyes.

10 Make the bows from pink and pale
blue dough. For each, roll out the dough
on a floured surface to ¼in (5mm) thick.
Cut a strip ½in (1cm) wide and 1½in (4cm)
long, and then cut to shape. Push into the
dough with the shaping tool to form the
knot, and mark little creases on either
side of it.

11 Make 17 small eggs, using all the
colours. For each, roll a ½-finger of dough
into a ball, and then gently roll one side
between your fingers to make it thinner.

12 Bake in the oven for 2 hours, until
crusted. Wearing oven gloves, remove
the glass and bake for a further 8–10
hours, until rock hard.

Finishing
13 When cold, decorate the eggs and
varnish the figure.

Easter hen

A big fat hen sits on her nest of Easter eggs. Her tummy is hollow so that you can hide the eggs underneath. She is painted after baking.

Materials
1½lb (750g) of plain dough (refer to Better
  Techniques)
6in (15cm) bowl
Silver foil to cover bowl
Stiff card
Silver foil/non-stick baking paper

Preparation
1 Turn the bowl upside down and cover it with silver foil. Fold the foil over the rim to secure it.

2 Trace the feather and crown stencils given here on to card and cut out.

Working the design
3 Roll out a large handful of dough to ½in (1cm) thick and large enough to cover the bowl. Lift it over the bowl and trim the edges. Bake in the oven at 175°F (80°C/gas mark ¼) for at least 2 hours. Remove the bowl and foil, and place the dough bowl upside down on silver foil/ baking paper. Do not leave it to cool down.

4 For the head, roll a palm of dough into a ball between your palms. Pinch one side between fingers and thumb to shape the beak.

5 For the tail, roll a ½-palm of dough, shape to a point between fingers and thumb, and attach to the opposite side.

6 Bake for at least 1 hour at 175°F (80°C/ gas mark ¼) to fix head and tail in place. Do not leave it to cool down.

7 To make the feathers, roll out a handful of dough to ⅛in (2.5mm) thick.

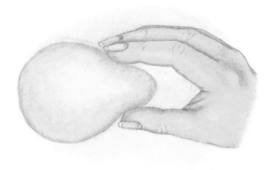

Mould the beak with your fingers

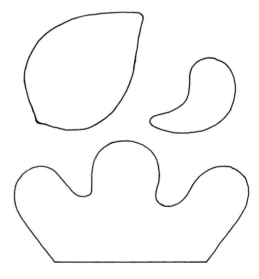

Trace the feather and crown shapes on to card and cut out

Place the feather stencil on the dough and cut round it with a small knife. Make as many feathers as you need to cover the whole hen except for the head.

8 Starting at the tail, fix the feathers in place so that they overlap slightly, working round the sides and towards the front.

9 Cut out the crown using the crown stencil and position it on top of the head.

10 Bake for 10 hours, or until rock hard.

Finishing
11 When cold, paint the features and varnish the hen.

Wedding couple

This wedding couple make an ideal gift for a bride and groom on their wedding day. It is made with plain and coloured dough and hangs on the wall.

Materials
2lb (1kg) of plain dough (refer to Better
 Techniques)
Paints or food dyes: red, pink, green,
 yellow
4 small plastic sandwich bags
Stiff card
Silver foil/non-stick baking paper
Garlic press

Preparation
1 Take a palm of dough and divide into
4 pieces. Knead one colour into each and
store in the plastic bags (refer to Better
Techniques).

2 Trace the flower stencil given here on
to card and cut out.

Working the design
3 For the bodies take 2 large handfuls of
dough and roll them into oblongs
$4\frac{1}{4} \times 1\frac{1}{2}$in (11 × 4cm). Place side by side on
silver foil/baking paper and push gently
so that they stick together. Cut off $\frac{3}{4}$in
(1.5cm) across the bottom.

4 Make 2 heads using $\frac{1}{2}$-palm of dough
for each, and roll into balls between your
palms. Place them above the bodies,
gently pressing down.

5 The groom: Mark out his jacket and
trousers with a shaping tool.

6 For his feet, roll 2 fingers of dough
into balls and push them up against his
trouser legs.

7 For his arms, roll a piece of dough into

a sausage and cut it in half on the
diagonal. Place one piece against the side
of his body and the other across his
chest. Cut both arms off at the wrists to
make sleeves. Roll 2 small balls of dough
for his hands and attach to the ends of
his sleeves.

Mark the jacket and trousers with a shaping tool

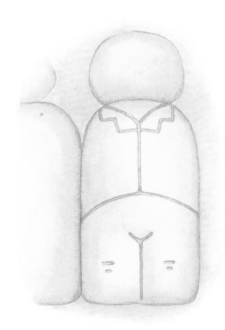

8 For his hair, push pieces of dough
through the garlic press and attach to the
top of his head. His ear is a pea-sized
piece of dough pressed against the side of
his head using the shaping tool.

9 The bride: Roll out a handful of dough $\frac{1}{8}$in (2.5mm) thick and wide enough to make the fullness of the skirt.

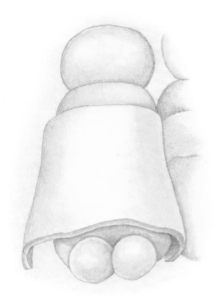

Cut out a piece of dough for the skirt

10 Place the skirt across her tummy and fold pleats into it by pushing the shaping tool up underneath it between two fingers.

Pinch dough over a shaping tool to form the pleats

11 Make the frill from a strip of dough 5$\frac{1}{2}$in (14cm) wide and $\frac{3}{4}$in (1.5cm) deep. Make pleats as for the skirt and then press it into the dough with the shaping tool to secure it.

12 Make her shoes, arms and hands in the same way as the groom's, and fold her inner arm over his.

13 Her hair is made using the garlic press. Attach the strands around her shoulders and work up around her face.

14 Use the red and pink dough for the flowers, making 8 pink flowers and 6 red. Roll out a piece of dough to $\frac{1}{4}$in (5mm) thick. Place the stencil on top and cut round with a small knife. To position a flower, place it on your fingers and press into the middle with a blunt pencil, then place it where you want it. Roll a tiny ball of dough and place it in the centre of the flower.

15 Fix a small piece of dough to the bride's stomach to make a platform on which the flowers can sit. Position 7 pink flowers across it and one on her hair. Then position 4 red flowers on her stomach, 1 on her hair, and one on the groom's jacket pocket.

16 Make 8 leaves from the green dough. Roll pea-sized pieces of dough into a ball and press to make oblongs. Position them around the flowers, and then press into them with the shaping tool to make the central veins.

17 Bake for 12 hours, or until rock hard, inserting the hook after 2 hours (refer to Basic Techniques).

Finishing
18 When cold, paint the couple's features and the details of their clothes, and varnish the whole.

Trace the flower on to card and cut out

FOUR

Animals and Dolls

Nellie the elephant

Nellie the elephant is ideal for those who have not done any dough modelling before. She is made with plain dough and painted afterwards, and hangs on the wall.

Materials
1½lb (750g) of plain dough (refer to Better Techniques)
Silver foil/non-stick baking paper
Toothpick
Hook

Working the design
1 For the body, take a handful of dough and roll it between your palms to make a fat oblong 3½in (9cm) long. Place it on the silver foil/baking paper.

2 For the head, take a palm of dough and roll it into a ball between your palms. Place it on the left-hand end of the oblong.

3 For the legs, roll a fat sausage of dough 4in (10cm) long and 1in (2cm) wide, and cut it in half on the diagonal. Position the legs below the body so that they point inwards.

4 Make each ear from a ½-finger of dough. Flatten the dough in the palm of your hand and place on a lightly floured surface. Cut out the ear shapes. Tuck the left ear (as you look at it) behind the head, and attach the right ear to the side of the head using a shaping tool.

5 Make the trunk from a sausage of dough rolled to 2¼in (6cm) long. Cut off one end on the diagonal and position it with the cut end flat against the head. Shape the other end with the shaping tool. Make the eyes with the toothpick.

Position the legs at an angle

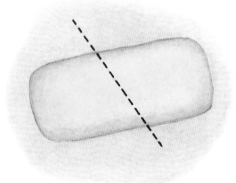

Make the legs

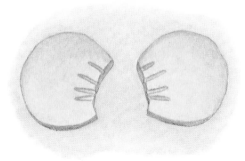

Cut out 2 pieces of dough for the ears

6 Make the tail from a small sausage of dough rolled to 1½in (4cm) long and ¼in (5mm) thick, and lay it across the end of the body fixing it neatly to the edge of the body shape. Fix a pea-sized oblong of dough to the end of the tail and flatten it with the shaping tool.

7 Bake in the oven for 10 hours or until rock hard, adding the hook after 2 hours (refer to Better Techniques).

Finishing
8 When cold, paint and add the features, and varnish.

Three little pigs

The first little pig built his house of straw, the second little pig built his house of wood and the third little pig built his house of brick.

Materials
1lb (500g) of plain dough (refer to Better
  Techniques)
Silver foil/non-stick baking paper
Garlic press
Toothpick
Small straw
Hook

Working the design
1 Use a palm of dough for each body
and roll between your palms into a fat
oblong. Place them side by side on silver
foil/baking paper and push them together
gently so that they stick.

2 Use a $\frac{1}{2}$-palm of dough for each head,
and roll between your palms into balls.
Place them on top of the bodies, pressing
them down gently.

3 Each pair of legs is made from a small
finger of dough. Roll into fat oblongs,
and cut off $\frac{1}{8}$in (2.5mm) across the top
and place below the bodies. Mark the
legs and trotters using a shaping tool.

4 Each nose is made from a fingertip of
dough. Roll into oblongs and mark two
nostrils on each using the end of a straw.
For the ears cut 6 small triangles from a
thin piece of dough. Attach to the sides
of their heads and fold the tips over.
Make the eyes with the toothpick.

5 For the arms, roll a piece of dough into a
sausage 3in (8cm) long between your palms
and cut into 4 pieces on the diagonal.

Mark the legs with a shaping tool

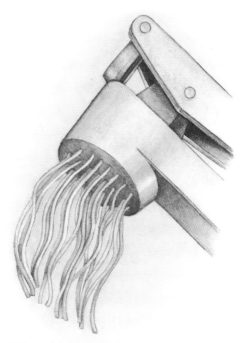

Make the straw with a garlic press

Position them on the outside figures and on each side of the middle figure.

6 Press a piece of dough through the garlic press to make the straw and postion it between the arms of the middle pig. Fix a little sausage of dough across the middle of the bundle of straw. For the pieces of wood, cut 3 strips of dough and pile them on top of the arm of the left-hand pig. The brick is a thick oblong of dough.

7 Bake for about 8 hours or until rock hard, adding the hook after 2 hours of baking (refer to Better Techniques).

Finishing
8 When cold, paint the wood, straw and brick, and varnish.

Baby bear with balloon

This bear floating along under his balloon looks lovely hanging in a child's room, and is a very good model for beginners as it is easy to make.

Materials
1lb (500g) of plain dough (refer to Better
   Techniques)
Silver foil/non-stick baking paper
Toothpick
Hook
Paperclip
8in (20cm) piece of gold string

Working the design
1 For the body, take a handful of dough and roll it between your palms into a ball. Then roll it gently into a fat oblong. Place it on silver foil/baking paper.

2 For the head, roll a palm of dough between your palms into a ball and place it above the body. Press it down gently to secure it to the body.

3 For the legs, roll a palm of dough between your palms into a sausage 4in (10cm) long and 1½in (4cm) thick, and cut in half on the diagonal. Position one leg directly below the body and the other so that it sticks out at an angle, with the cut ends against the body piece.

4 For the arms, roll a palm of dough between your palms into a sausage 3½in (9cm) long and 1in (2cm) thick. Cut in half on the diagonal and attach to the body.

5 Shape a bean-sized piece of dough for each ear and press them into the head using a shaping tool. Use a small fingertip of dough for the muzzle and a pea-sized piece for the nose. Make the eyes with a toothpick.

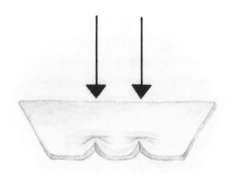

Cut out a piece of dough for the bow tie

6 To make the bow tie, roll out a small piece of dough on a floured surface to ¼in (5mm) thick. Cut a strip ½in (1cm) wide and 1½in (4cm) long, and then cut to shape. Push into the dough with the

Cut a sausage of dough in half for the legs

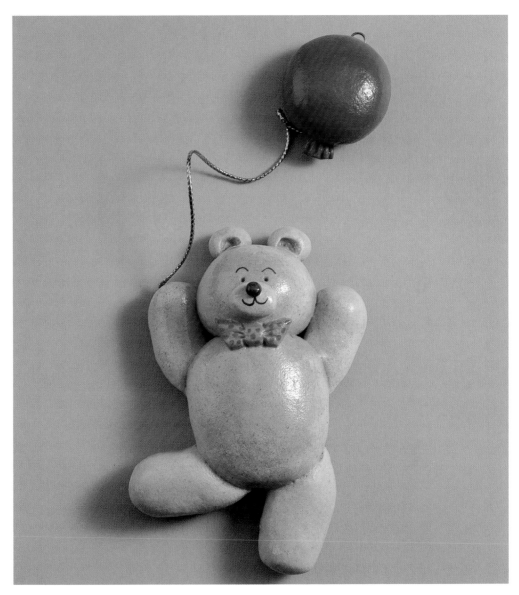

shaping tool to form the knot, and mark little creases on either side of it. Position on the bear's neck.

7 Make the balloon from a small handful of dough. Roll it into a ball between your palms and flatten it slightly with the palm of your hand. Attach a pea-sized piece of dough to one side of it and flatten it using the shaping tool. Press some lines into the balloon around the tie with the shaping tool.

8 Bake for 10 hours or until rock hard, adding the hook to the back of the bear and pushing the paperclip into the balloon after 2 hours (refer to Better Techniques).

Finishing
9 When cold, paint the bear's features, the bow tie and balloon, and varnish the whole bear. Glue one end of the gold string to the back of the balloon and the other to the back of the bear's hand.

Clown

This bright, happy clown is full of colour.
He hangs on the wall, stirring memories of the circus
and bringing a smile to all who see him.

Materials
2lb (1kg) of plain dough (refer to Better
   Techniques)
Silver foil/non-stick baking paper
Toothpick
Hook

Working the design
1 For the body, roll a handful of dough
into a rounded oblong and flatten it
slightly with the palm of your hand. Place
on silver foil/baking paper.

2 For the legs, roll a fat sausage of dough
between your palms, and cut in half on
the diagonal. Position below the body,
and cut off across the bottom to form
trousers.

3 For each boot, roll a ¼-palm of dough
between your palms into an oblong wide
enough to fit the trouser legs and ¾in
(1.5cm) deep. Press them gently against

the bottom of the trousers. Roll 2 balls
from a ¼-palm of dough each and press
against the bottom of the legs.

4 For the coat, roll out a palm of dough
to approximately 4 × ¾in (10 × 1.5cm), and
cut out 2 coat pieces. To position them,
attach down the back first, and fold over
to the front of the body. The pockets are
made from 2 ¾in (1.5cm) squares of
dough ⅛in (2.5mm) thick, and placed on
the coat.

5 Make the nose from a large pea-sized
piece of dough, and make the eyes with
the toothpick.

6 For the hat, roll a ½-palm of dough to
2¼ × 2in (6 × 5cm) and ⅛in (2.5mm) thick.
Cut out the hat shape and place round
the top of the head, pinching the tip and
folding it over sideways. Use a shaping
tool to mark the brim, and attach a large
pea-sized piece of dough to the tip.

7 For the arms, roll a sausage of dough
between your palms and cut in half on

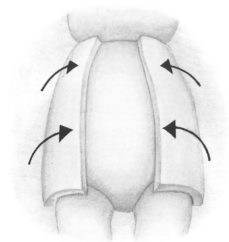

Cut out 2 pieces of dough for the coat

Cut out a piece of dough for the hat

62

the diagonal. Place them by his head and cut across the ends to form sleeves.

8 For each ear, roll out a tiny round of dough and press against the side of the head with the shaping tool.

9 Roll 2 small balls of dough between your palms for the hands and attach to the sleeves. Press into the hands with the shaping tool to create the thumbs.

10 For the bow tie, roll out the dough to $\frac{1}{4}$in (5mm) thick. Cut a strip $\frac{1}{2}$in (1cm) wide and $1\frac{1}{2}$in (4cm) long, and then cut to shape. Push into the dough with the

shaping tool to form the knot, and mark little creases on either side of it. Position on his neck, and press round the top of the coat pieces to form the neckband.

11 Make the buttons from 2 small pieces of dough rolled into balls, and place on his stomach.

12 Bake for 10 hours or until rock hard, adding the hook after 2 hours of baking (refer to Better Techniques).

Finishing
13 When cold, paint his clothes and features, and varnish the whole clown.

Rag doll

This rag doll is an ideal present for a young girl. Instead of flowers at her feet you could put the girl's name, turning it into a bedroom door plate.

Materials
1½lb (750g) of plain dough (refer to Better Techniques)
Silver foil/non-stick baking paper
Garlic press
3in (8cm) pastry cutter
Stiff card
Toothpick

Preparation
1 Trace the flower shape given here on to card and cut out.

Working the design
2 For the body, roll a handful of dough between your palms into an oblong 4 × 1½in (10 × 4cm), and place on silver foil/baking paper. Cut off ½in (1cm) across the bottom. Make 2 small balls for her

feet and attach them. Attach a wide oval-shaped piece of dough below her feet for the flowers.

3 For the head, roll a ½-palm of dough into a ball between your palms. Place above the body and press down gently to attach it. Add a tiny ball of dough for her nose.

4 For the dress, measure across the stomach for the width and add on a little extra, then measure from just below the neckline to the toes for the length. Roll out a piece of dough to these measurements plus ¼in (5mm) all round. Cut out the shape of the dress. Carefully lift the dress into place, positioning it about ½in (1cm) below the neckline. With a shaping tool, press the dress against the body round the top to form a waistband.

Cut out a piece of dough for the skirt

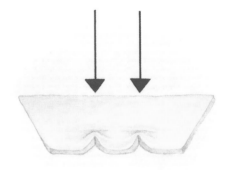

Cut out a piece of dough for the bow

5 To make the bow, roll out a piece of dough on a floured surface to ¼in (5mm) thick. Cut a strip ½in (1cm) wide and 1½in (4cm) long, and then cut to shape. Push

into the dough with the shaping tool to form the knot, and mark little creases on either side of it. Position in the middle of the waistband. Cut out 2 narrow strips of dough for the ribbons and position under the bow.

6 For the arms, roll a sausage of dough between your palms. Cut in half on the diagonal and position on either side of the body with the cut ends against the body piece.

7 Push pieces of dough through the garlic press for the hair and attach it starting at the shoulders and working up to the top of the head.

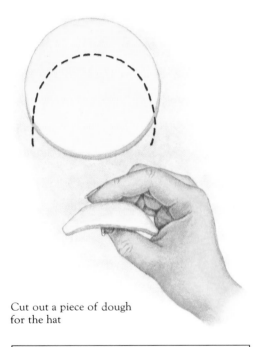

Cut out a piece of dough
for the hat

8 For the hat, roll out a piece of dough to ½in (1cm) thick, and cut out a piece with the pastry cuter. Cut out a half-moon shape from this for the brim and fix round the top of the head. For the crown, take an oblong of dough, press it up in the middle and place behind the brim.

9 For the teddy bear, roll a ¼-finger of dough into a ball for the body. Use pieces half that size for the head, legs and arms. Roll tiny balls for the nose and ears, and make the eyes with the toothpick. The bear's face is quite fiddly, so make sure the dough is not too sticky.

Trace the flower on to card and cut out

10 Make 8 flowers. Roll out a piece of dough to ¼in (5mm) thick. Place the flower stencil on top and cut round with a small knife. To position a flower, place it on your closed fingers and press into the middle with a blunt pencil, then place it where you want it. Roll a tiny ball of dough and place it in the centre of the flower.

11 Bake for 10 hours or until rock hard, adding the hook after 2 hours (refer to Better Techniques).

Finishing
12 When cold, paint the girl's clothes and flowers, paint in the features on her and the teddy's face, and varnish the whole.

66

Pen-holder doll

This little doll reading a book is perfect for decorating a young girl's room and helping to keep it tidy. It is made from plain dough and painted afterwards.

Materials

2lb (1kg) of plain dough (refer to Better
   Techniques)
Stiff card
Straight-sided round glass, oiled
Silver foil/non-stick baking paper
Toothpick
Garlic press
4in (10cm) pastry cutter

Preparation

1 Trace the flower shape given here on to
card and cut out.

Working the design

2 Take a large handful of dough and roll
out to ¼in (5mm) thick, 5in (13cm) long
and wide enough to fold round the oiled
glass.

3 Place the glass on its side. Wet the two
long sides of the piece of dough, wrap the
dough around the glass and press the two
sides together to join them firmly.

4 Cut out a circle of dough ¼in (5mm)
thick slightly larger than the bottom of
the glass. Stand the glass on it and press
them together. Stand on a baking tray
and bake for at least 2 hours, until the
dough has crusted.

5 Wearing oven gloves, remove from the
oven and leave to cool for about 15
minutes (so that the dough does not
shrink and crack). Gently twist the glass
and remove from the dough.

6 Place the pen-holder on silver foil/
baking paper and wet the area against
which the doll will sit. For the body, take
a palm of dough and roll between your
palms to make a fat sausage
approximately 2¾in (7cm) long. Using
your thumb, press the dough into a
sitting position, and place it against the
part-baked pen-holder.

7 For the head, take a ½-palm of dough
and roll into a ball between your palms.
Place on top of the body and press down
gently so that it sticks to the body.

8 For the legs, roll a sausage of dough
between your palms 4¾in (12cm) long and
¾in (1.5cm) thick. Cut it in half on the
diagonal and attach to the body. Roll
small pieces of dough for the feet and
press against the ends of the legs. Use a
shaping tool to make the socks.

9 For the dress, measure across the
stomach for the width and add on a little
extra, then measure from just below the
neckline to the toes for the length. Roll
out a piece of dough to these
measurements plus ¼in (5mm) all round.

Cut out a piece of dough for the skirt

Cut out the shape of the dress. Carefully lift the dress into place, positioning it about ½in (1cm) below the neckline. Press it against the body round the top with the shaping tool, to form a waistband and spread it out around the doll.

10 For the waistband, roll out a strip of dough to ¼in (5mm) thick and long enough to wrap around the stomach. Press into place with your fingers.

11 For the arms, roll a sausage of dough 4¾in (12cm) long and about ¾in (1.5cm) thick. Cut it in half on the diagonal and attach to the body. Cut off the ends and attach small balls of dough for the hands.

12 For the hair, push pieces of dough through the garlic press. Attach hair starting at the shoulders and working up to the top of the head.

13 For the hat, roll out a piece of dough to ½in (1cm) thick, and cut out a circle with the pastry cutter. Cut out a half-moon shape from this for the brim and fix round the top of the head. For the crown, take an oblong of dough, press it up in the middle and place behind the brim. Make the hatband in the same way as the waistband.

14 Make 2 flowers. Roll out a piece of dough to ¼in (5mm) thick. Place the flower stencil on top and cut round with a small knife. To position a flower, place it on your finger and press into the middle with a blunt pencil, then place it where you want it. Roll a tiny ball of dough and place it in the centre of the flower.

Trace the flower on to card and cut out

15 For the book, roll out a finger of dough to ⅛in (2.5mm) thick and cut out a piece 2 × 1in (5 × 2cm). Use the shaping tool to mark out the book binding and place on top of the hands.

16 Roll a tiny piece of dough into a ball for the nose. Make the eyes with a toothpick.

17 Bake for 10 hours or until rock hard.

Finishing
18 When cold, paint the doll's clothes and the features on her face, paint and decorate the pen-holder, and varnish.

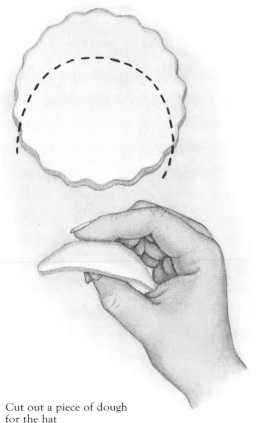

Cut out a piece of dough for the hat

69

Lucky fish

This pretty charm of two entwined fish may look complicated, but it is easy to model, and will bring you good luck. It is painted at the end.

Materials
1½lb (750g) of plain dough (refer to Better
    Techniques)
Stiff card
Silver foil/non-stick baking paper
Small straw

Preparation
1 Trace the fish tail stencil given here on
to card and cut out.

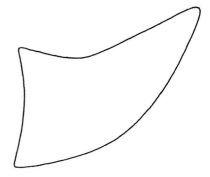

Working the design
2 Take 2 handfuls of dough and shape
into 2 fat sausages. Roll one end of each
thinner, and curve them around so that 1
fish faces up and 1 down. Place on silver
foil/baking paper.

Trace the fish tail on to card and cut out

3 For the tails, roll out a piece of dough
to ½in (1cm) thick. Place the tail stencil on
top and cut round with a small knife.
Make 4 tail pieces and position them
around the fish.

4 Cut out a circle of dough 2¼in (6cm) in
diameter. Cut in half and put a half on
each fish's back. Use the shaping tool to
mark scales and indentations on the fish.

5 Make the eyes by rolling a small pea-
sized piece of dough for each and
flattening them slightly. Press into each
with the end of a straw to make the
eyeballs. Make the mouth by rolling a
pea-sized piece of dough out thinly for
each and curling it into a circle.

Arrange the body pieces in an S-shape with the
tail sections joined

6 Bake for 8–10 hours, or until rock
hard.

Finishing
7 When cold, paint and decorate the
fish, and varnish.

Necklace

Salt dough can even be used to create delicate pieces of jewelry. Sun, moon, stars and beads are all made from dough for this lovely necklace.

Materials

1lb (500g) of plain dough (refer to Better
   Techniques)
Stiff card
Silver foil/non-stick baking paper
Small straw
7 jewelry hooks
Leather rope

Preparation

1 Trace the large and small stars and
moon stencils given here on to card and
cut out.

Working the design

2 Roll out a handful of dough. Place the
large star stencil on top of dough and cut
out with a small knife. Transfer on to
silver foil/baking paper. Use a shaping
tool to edge the star shape.

3 Take 2 bean-sized pieces of dough, and
place on the star. Use the end of the
straw to make the eyeballs. Make the
mouth from another bean-sized piece of
dough rolled out thinly. Shape the mouth
with the shaping tool. Make the nose
from a bean-sized piece of dough shaped
into a triangle. Shape the eyebrows with
the shaping tool.

4 Roll out a palm of dough and cut out 2
moon shapes and 4 small star shapes, and
place on the silver foil/baking paper.

5 Make the beads by rolling 4 small balls
of dough between a finger and the palm
of your hand. Push the small straw
through the middle of each to make a
hole, and place the beads on the silver
foil/baking paper.

6 Bake for $\frac{1}{2}$ hour. Remove from oven
and insert the jewelry hooks into the tops
of the stars and moons. Continue baking
for another $3\frac{1}{2}$ hours or until rock hard.

Finishing

7 When cold, paint and varnish all the
items. Thread them on to the leather
rope, tying a knot between each to hold
them in place.

Decorate the edge of the big star

Trace the star and moon
shapes on to card and
cut out

Better Techniques

❧

Everything you need to know about salt-dough preparation – the tools of the trade, useful hints to help you, illustrations to guide you, and what to do if things go wrong.

MAKING SALT DOUGH

The following quantities are based on 1lb (500g) of flour:

1lb (500g) of plain, unbleached flour
½lb (250g) of salt
2 tablespoons of oil
½pt (300ml) of water

Place the flour and salt in a bowl and mix them together. Then add the oil and water and mix to form a firm dough. This is best done in an electric mixer with a dough hook. Otherwise use your hands.

To tell when the dough is ready for use: If it sticks to the sides of the bowl (or to your hands), it contains too much water – add more flour until it leaves the sides of the bowl clean. If it is crumbly, or cracks when you roll it, it is too dry – gradually add more water, 2 tablespoons at a time, until it is the correct consistency.

Store the dough in a plastic bag until you are ready to use it. Take out as much as you need, knead it roughly into shape and then roll it between your hands or roll out with a rolling-pin. When rolling out a piece of dough, work on a lightly floured surface. The dough shouldn't be sticky for making small pieces.

BASIC MATERIALS AND EQUIPMENT

Salt dough is made from flour, salt, water and oil, and should always be well kneaded before use. In addition, there are a few basic tools that are needed for all the projects, although the shaping tool is the only one that you may need to get especially for dough modelling.

Unbleached plain flour

A 3lb (1.4kg) bag of plain, unbleached flour will make enough dough for a variety of exciting models. Unbleached flour contains more starch than other types, which makes modelling easier.

Salt

Ordinary household cooking salt will do, preferably extra fine.

Water

This is very important. Not only is it used in making the dough, it is also the gluing agent for sticking each part in place. A water spray is very useful.

Oil

Oil does not help to preserve salt dough, but it does prevent the wet dough from splitting. It also protects your hands from becoming too dry when mixing up lots of dough.

Kitchen bowl

The salt dough mixture can be made in a

mixing bowl or washing-up bowl. Rubber gloves will protect your hands because the salt in the dough can make your knuckles sore after a lot of kneading. If you have a food-processor with a dough-making attachment, this can save a lot of hard work.

Silver foil or non-stick baking paper

Assemble the dough figures on a sheet of silver foil or baking paper as this will make it easy to transfer them to a baking tray. It also prevents the dough from sticking to the baking tray. If you want to re-use a piece of silver foil/baking paper, bake the model for at least 2 hours. Then, wearing oven gloves, carefully peel away the foil/paper and return the model to the baking tray.

Shaping tool

This is the only item that has to be bought especially for making salt-dough models. It is used for making indentations and creases on clothes, flowers, leaves, and so on, and for positioning the trickier pieces of dough.

Rolling-pin

This is used in several of the projects. A child's rolling-pin is ideal for rolling small pieces of dough. Always roll out the dough on a lightly floured surface.

Kitchen knife

Use a small, pointed knife with a sharp edge for cutting out shapes in the dough.

Garlic press

This is used for making hair, grass, trees, and so on. Place a blob of dough in the crusher and push down. Cut off the strands with a sharp knife.

Straws and toothpicks

Straws are used for making holes and indentations in the dough. Press into the dough and twist. The dough should come out in the straw. The toothpick is also used pressed into the dough. You can make a hole by twisting it in a circle.

Felt-tip pen and biro lids

These are ideal tools for making patterns on garments and flowers. Look for ones with interesting patterns in the lid.

Pastry cutters

These are excellent for cutting out thin pieces of dough, for example for Christmas tree decorations.

BASIC BODY ASSEMBLY

Water is the gluing agent. Wet the areas of dough to be joined and press them together gently so that they stick. A plant-spray such as the type found in garden centres is ideal for this. Attach each part as you go, in the order given in the instructions.

BAKING THE MODELS

The dough models are baked in the oven. This is used at such a low temperature that it is much cheaper than using a kiln. If you need to cook a meal, you can take the dough model out and replace it afterwards. In this case, you must keep the model warm – in a top oven (it does not have to be on) or by covering it with towels – or it will crack when it is returned to the oven.

When using an oven that is not fan-assisted, place freshly made dough in the bottom of the oven. As you raise the oven temperature, raise the dough from the bottom to the middle tray. If, after the estimated baking time, the dough is still a bit soft, turn it over and bake for longer.

To test if the model is rock hard, tap the back. If it sounds hollow, it needs longer in the oven: if it sounds like tapping on brick it is ready.

The dough models should always be allowed to cool down slowly, or the flatter pieces in particular may crack as they cool. Either turn off the oven and leave them in there, or take them out and wrap in a cloth until cold.

Oven temperatures
Newly-made models – 175°F (80°C/ gas mark ¼).
After 2 hours – 200°F (100°C/gas mark ¼).
After 6 hours – 250°F (120°C/gas mark ¼).

If you would like the dough to brown, raise the temperature to 350°F (180°C/gas mark 4), but do keep checking the oven every 5 minutes until the desired colour is reached.

If you plan to leave the oven on overnight, leave it at 200°F (100°C/ gas mark ¼).

INSERTING THE HOOK
Many of the models hang from a hook hidden in the back. These are best made from garden wire bent into a loop.

Bake the figure for at least 2 hours, or until the surface has safely set. Wearing oven gloves, carefully tip the figure front down on to your left hand and peel back the silver foil/baking paper. Push the looped wire downwards into the back of the model, and return it to the oven.

Once the figure has baked and been allowed to cool, give the hook a good tug to make sure it is not loose in the dough. If it is loose, this is a fairly good indication that the dough is not solid all the way through. Return it to the oven and bake for longer. You can add a few drops of a very strong glue to the hook for extra protection.

Forgetting to insert the hook
This is easily done. The best remedy for larger figures sounds a bit drastic – use a drill! Carefully lay the figure on to a towel and drill into the back, making sure the hole is large enough to take a large nail, and that it is high enough up the figure so that it hangs straight without sliding sideways. Also remember that the dough has two different strengths. The surface is very strong and is harder to drill through than the middle, so be prepared for a sudden breakthrough, and make sure you don't drill right through to the front by mistake. If you are unhappy about using a drill, please ask somebody who is used to using one. Smaller figures can be fixed to a wall with double-sided sticky pads.

PAINTING THE MODELS
The dough can either be used plain and painted after baking, or it can be coloured before use. A model should be left to go cold before painting.

Painting
Painting dough models makes them much more realistic. Poster paints come in bright colours and are easy to use. They are also non-toxic, so are suitable for children to use. All you do is put a ¼-teaspoon of paint in a painter's palette and gradually add small amounts of water until you get the consistency you like. If you add too much water, the paint will not be bright, so add more paint.

Two sizes of paint brush are useful: an average size (no. 5) and a thin brush (no. 0). Use the soft-bristle variety.

Colouring the dough
Dough can be coloured with either poster paints or food dyes. Use roughly the amount of dough needed.

For a bright colour use poster paints, which also hold the colour better once baked. Gently knead a finger of paint into the dough until it is evenly mixed in; add more if you want a brighter colour. A ¼-teaspoon of colour will give enough paint for a large handful of dough.

When using food dyes, you will find that the dough will become a lot softer, so add more flour. The colours are not as bright as the poster paints, but they give a nice, natural effect. Add the food dye drop by drop until you have the colour you want. Remember to wear protective gloves when using food dyes as they stain your hands and clothes.

Colour chart
1 part red + 3 parts white – pink
1 part blue + 3 parts red – purple
2 parts yellow + 1 part blue – green
2 parts yellow + 1 part red – orange
3 parts black + 1 part white – grey
1 part orange + 2 parts white – peach
For pale colours add white.

VARNISING
Use clear varnish, the thicker the better. To test for the thickest one, just shake the cans. Use a painter's brush to apply the varnish, and make sure that all sides are varnished. If you use a thin, watery varnish, apply several coats. Always varnish the back and front of a model as it helps to keep moisture out.

TROUBLE-SHOOTING
There are various ways of saving a model that seems to be going wrong.

Blistering (air bubbles)
This means that the oven is too hot. First reduce the temperature. Using a water spray, wet the bubble and prick it. Then gently press out the air using your fingers and smooth over the surface. If the surface dough is too hard to do this, break the blister and fill it with fresh dough.

Parts fall off
Insufficient water has been used when sticking the parts together. Either use some fresh dough to bind the two sections together, or use a glue (wood glue or a similar type).

Cracking and splitting
This tends to happen across large, flattish areas, probably because the dough is too wet. Dough expands while baking and contracts again while cooling, causing the dough to split. If you reduce the proportion of water in the mixture, this will mean less expansion and therefore less contraction.

Another method of preventing cracking is to slow down the cooling down process. Either turn off the oven once the figures are rock hard and leave them in it to cool down gradually, or, if you have to take them out, wrap them in a towel and leave them in a warmish place.

LEFTOVER DOUGH
Sometimes you will find that there is some dough left over. It is a good idea to store it and use it for mending any broken parts or for filling cracks and holes. Unbaked dough makes an excellent gluing agent. Another idea for using up extra dough is to make small fridge magnets, or maybe even gifts to put into children's party bags. Roll out the dough quite thin and cut out shapes using animal pastry cutters. If you would like them to hang, either insert a paper clip (silver one) after $\frac{1}{2}$ hour of baking, or make a hole with a straw and thread them on to string, or glue a small magnet (usually found in craft shops) to the back after baking.

Dough will last in a plastic bag for a day. Once it becomes sticky, either add more flour, or make a fresh batch.

CARING FOR SALT-DOUGH FIGURES
Salt dough is made from organic products and needs to be preserved and cared for. If you do this, your models will last forever. They should be kept dry and free from moisture at all times. Check that they are not left on a window ledge, where condensation may occur, near damp walls, or out of doors. If they get wet, the dough will become soggy and expand, eventually splitting and rotting.

Storing Christmas decorations

Christmas decorations are best stored wrapped in tissue paper in a box. Do not store them in plastic wrapping, because they may sweat in the heat. Please do not store them in a garage or loft because the temperature changes too dramatically in such places.

If they go soft

If a salt-dough figure has been left somewhere damp, but hasn't lost its shape, it is possible to restore it.

Leave it in an airing cupboard until it is rock hard or in a warm oven with the door open. Make sure the heat does not burn the varnish. Once the figure is rock hard, re-varnish it on both sides.

Cleaning

Do not use polish or any other spray cleaners on salt-dough figures. A dry cloth is all that is needed.

FLOWERS

Flowers can be made either by using a stencil to cut out a flower shape, for a flat flower, or by modelling them.

Using a flower stencil

To make a flower stencil, trace the flower on to a piece of stiff card and cut it out. Place the cut-out on a $\frac{1}{4}$in (5mm) thick piece of rolled dough and cut round it using a small, sharp knife or scalpel. Place the flower on your fingers and press into the middle with a blunt pencil. This should make the petals fold up and inwards slightly. Then, leaving the flower on the pencil, press it into place where you want it. Remove the pencil. Roll a pea-sized piece of dough into a ball and place it in the centre of the flower.

Modelling flowers

Primrose shape: Flatten 5 pea-size pieces of dough between your fingers. Place them around the flower centre, which is a small, thin sausage of dough. Fold the petals around the thin sausage.

Rose shape: Roll out a piece of dough to $\frac{1}{16}$in (1mm) thick and cut a strip $\frac{1}{2}$in

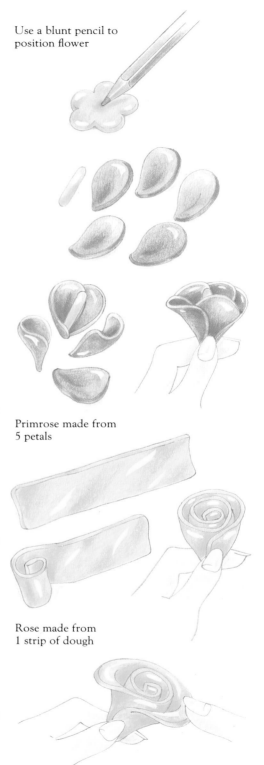

Use a blunt pencil to position flower

Primrose made from 5 petals

Rose made from 1 strip of dough

Plain flower press

Using a garlic press

Using a straw

Shaping a sun

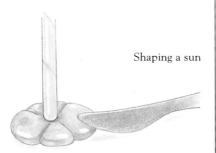

Shaping a flower

(1cm) wide and 1½in (4cm) long. Using your finger, gently roll up the strip of dough. With your fingertips, carefully separate the layers of petals. Place the end of a toothpick into the centre of the flower and press the flower into position on the figure. Make a small hole so that the rose sits nicely.

Leaves
Form the dough into a rounded oblong and flatten it between your finger and thumb. Use your fingertips to form the tip of the leaf. Make the central vein using a shaping tool.

FLOWER AND PATTERN PRESSES

Flower and pattern presses can be made from dough and used to decorate clothing, flowers and so on by pressing them into the dough figure.

Cut a strip of dough 1½in (4cm) long and ½in (1cm) thick, and roll it into a ball.

Roll a ball of dough the size of a bean. Press down gently on it to flatten it slightly, and then use a garlic press to press some dough into it. Cut the strands of dough to make them ¼in (5mm) long.

Roll a ball of dough the size of a bean and press down gently to flatten it slightly. Press into the centre with the end of a straw.

Roll a ball of dough the size of a bean and press down gently to flatten it slightly. Mark a small circle in the middle and use a shaping tool to create a sun.

Roll a ball of dough the size of a bean and press down gently to flatten it slightly. Use a shaping tool to create a flower effect.

Bake the press for at least 4 hours or until rock hard. When cold, varnish it and glue it to the end of a pencil.

Acknowledgements

Thank you to everyone who encouraged me to write this book. To my very dear friends who have always helped me when it was needed, and especially to my two very special children, James and Olivia. Without all your help and understanding this book would never have been completed.